Original title:
Sprouting Love

Copyright © 2025 Creative Arts Management OÜ
All rights reserved.

Author: Natalia Harrington
ISBN HARDBACK: 978-1-80581-880-9
ISBN PAPERBACK: 978-1-80581-407-8
ISBN EBOOK: 978-1-80581-880-9

Echoes of the Season

In springtime's breeze, we dance so bright,
Butterflies giggle, what a funny sight.
Pollen's a prankster, tickling our nose,
Sneezing together, how the laughter grows.

Yellow daisies tease with whispers of cheer,
While bunnies hop around, full of good beer.
We toss silly flowers, laughter in the air,
Found in the chaos, a love so rare.

Dewdrops on New Beginnings

Morning dew glistens, a sparkling jest,
Each droplet a message, 'Blue jeans are best!'
As sunbeams chuckle, they warm our day,
Rolling in grass, we giggle and play.

With birdies tweeting their sweet little lines,
We prance through the tulips, in mismatched designs.
Coffee cups laughing, spills shared in jest,
In this quirky dance, we know we are blessed.

Rooted in Tranquility

Under the oak where shadows embrace,
Two squirrels debate about nuts in this place.
They chatter and giggle, oh what a show,
Our love finds its rhythm, like vines, they do grow.

With every soft rustle, a secret we share,
Whispers of nature float sweet through the air.
Roots deep in laughter, a fortress we build,
In our silly kingdom, our hearts are fulfilled.

Where Love Takes Root

In the garden of giggles, where wild things grow,
We plant all our dreams in a row after row.
Roses wear glasses, daisies in shoes,
What a delight, oh, we dance with the blues.

Puppies are barking, they're joining the fun,
Chasing their tails 'til the day is done.
With buckets of chuckles, we water our hearts,
Here in this laughter, true love never departs.

A Canvas of Color and Heart

In the garden, where we met,
You tripped on flowers, what a threat!
Petals flew, and so did cheer,
Nature giggled, loud and clear.

With paint-stained hands, we made our mark,
Splashed on colors, bright and stark.
A canvas filled with joy and glee,
You laughed as I slipped, oh dear me!

In tangled vines, our laughter grew,
Beehives buzzing, friends anew.
We danced around, what a sight,
Underneath the disco light.

So here's to blooms and mishaps fine,
In the chaos, your hand in mine.
With every bloom, our joy expands,
A palette drawn by funny hands.

In the Arms of Wildflowers

With daisies in your hair so bright,
You spun around, what a delight!
Caught a bumblebee mid-flight,
Squealed loudly, oh what a fright!

We raced the wind in silly strides,
Through the meadows, wildflower rides.
Tangled roots beneath our feet,
Fell in laughter, oh, what a feat!

Your hat flew off, a comical sight,
Chased it down with all my might.
In fields of color, stories told,
Each petal grinning, none too bold.

So let the blossoms wrap us tight,
In a dance that feels just right.
With nature's whimsy, we'll always play,
In the arms of blooms, we'll find our way.

Coloring the Canvas of Us

Your smile's a splash of bright red,
Like a paint blob on my bed.
We dance with brushes in our hands,
Creating colors, fun unplanned.

With each stroke, we giggle loud,
Art critics would be quite too proud.
Our hearts, they leap and twirl around,
In this wild gallery we've found.

Who knew love could be this bright?
Your quirky hat, a funny sight.
On this canvas, we have fun,
Two oddballs who become as one.

Tender Blooms Beneath the Sky

Beneath the clouds, our jokes take flight,
We plant our seeds, oh what a sight.
You picked a daisy for my ear,
Then told me puns that made me cheer.

With sunshine smiles, we make it rain,
A garden blossoming with no pain.
Your laugh's a flower, wild and free,
Growing petals just for me, you see?

We water dreams with silly songs,
Our leafy jokes, they can't be wrongs.
Beneath the sky, we laugh with glee,
Two crazy pots, just you and me.

Growing Stronger Together

In this patch, we plant the fun,
Your silly jokes weigh tons, oh hon!
We raise our flags of laughter high,
Two quirky plants reaching for the sky.

With roots so tangled and entwined,
We're the best team you could find.
You share the light, I'll soak the rain,
Growing strong through joy and pain.

Like vines that twist and stretch with glee,
Our playful hearts are wild and free.
Tending this garden, side by side,
In the humor of love, we take pride.

Tales of the Leafy Heart

In the forest of whims, we find our way,
You tell a tale that makes my day.
With leafy whispers and chuckles loud,
Under the trees, we laugh out proud.

A squirrel steals our picnic snacks,
We chase it down, avoiding cracks.
In this green world of silly quests,
Our love's the leaf that never rests.

With every twist and turn we take,
Your joking grin makes my heart ache.
In this leafy realm, full of cheer,
You're the punchline that I hold dear.

Nature's Vows

In the meadow, giggles roar,
Butterflies dance, wanting more.
A squirrel wedged between two trees,
Chasing dreams with expert ease.

Sunflowers nod, they've found a mate,
Petals whisper, it's never too late.
Bees hum soft, love's nectar bliss,
Cuddle bugs, a slippery kiss.

Cradled in the Earth

Under soil, while worms debate,
Roses argue who's first date.
A cactus pricks with jealous glee,
While vines entwine, oh look at me!

Earthworms waltz, with much delight,
While radishes glow in moonlight.
Underneath where secrets dwell,
Roots of joy begin to swell.

Love's Hidden Garden

Among the greens, they plot and scheme,
Dandelions burst in little beams.
A ladybug, her love on a leaf,
Sips morning dew, sharing belief.

Lettuce whispers, 'check my style,'
Radishes boasting of charm, oh so vile.
Garden gnomes chuckle with glee,
Watching chaos sprout effortlessly.

Fragile Tendrils Reaching Out

Vines shimmy, a silly dance,
Hoping to grab that one chance.
A floppy leaf, cries 'don't let go!'
While timid buds say, 'just say so!'

Laughter fills the air so light,
As tiny seeds take off in flight.
Tendrils twist, they want a hug,
Nature's warmth, like a cozy rug.

In the Garden of Us

In a patch where laughter grows,
We plant our quirks in neat little rows.
Watered with giggles, sun-kissed, we thrive,
In this green world, our jokes come alive.

The weeds are the worries, we'll pull them with glee,
We'll dance with the butterflies, just you and me.
With each sunflower smile, my heart skips a beat,
In our garden of chaos, there's joy at our feet.

Courage in the Cracks

In the sidewalk's crevice, a flower stands tall,
With courage and laughter, it dances through all.
It whispers to raindrops with a cheeky delight,
'Watch out, world! I've got a colorful fight!'

Each petal a giggle, each stem a bright pun,
Beneath pavement's pressure, we laugh and we run.
In the crevices wondering, how did you hide?
With humor in roots, nothing can divide!

Harmonious Growth

Two plants in a pot, oh, what a sight!
They wiggle and giggle, wrapped up so tight.
One says, 'I'm thirsty!' the other replies,
'Just drink from my laughter, it's sweetened surprise!'

Tangled up roots in a friendship so strong,
Together they sing a delightful song.
With leaves touching gently, they whisper and smile,
In this garden of joy, let's grow for a while.

The Language of Foliage

Oh, the leaves have stories, if you listen real close,
They gossip like children, each twig has a dose.
'Check out my new buds!' one leaf wiggles in glee,
'Heard it from a flower, everyone agrees!'

In this forest of chuckles, they trade secret jokes,
Between the bark's laughter, among the fine oaks.
Foliage is fun, with each branch a delight,
In the canopy life, everything's all right!

Hearts in Full Bloom

In the garden of giggles, we plant our dreams,
Watered with laughter, so silly it seems.
Petals of humor burst forth with a grin,
Honeybees buzzing, let the fun times begin!

Daisies in shades of bright yellow and red,
Tickle our noses, and dance in our head.
With each little bloom, my heart skips a beat,
Nature's own comedy, oh, how sweet!

The Promise of a New Season

Springtime arrives with a wink and a nod,
It tickles the flowers, calls them a clod.
Squirrels in bow ties, oh, what a sight!
They dance through the branches, from morning till night.

Old man winter, he's taking a snooze,
While the grass dons its finest bright hues.
Garden gnomes chuckle, they know what's in store,
More mischief and mirth—oh, we can't ask for more!

Lush Embraces

Two trees entwined, what a sight to behold,
Branches hugging tight, stories untold.
Their shadows are giggles, their leaves dance in glee,
Nature's own jester, as playful as can be.

The flowers gossip, sharing secrets so spunky,
While beetles do ballet, looking quite funky.
Amongst all this joy, I can't help but smile,
In the arms of the flora, let's stay here awhile!

Harmony in the Garden

In our lush little paradise, everything's clear,
The candy-colored blooms whisper sweet cheer.
Ladybugs chatter, spreading joy all around,
While the worms underground dance to the sound.

A parade of petals, with quirks full of flair,
Make way for the butterflies, float in the air.
With nature's own laughter, it's a party, you see,
In this comical haven, forever we'll be.

Embracing the Spring

The sun cracks jokes on the green grass,
While tulips giggle at a bee's pass.
Daisies whisper secrets, quite daring,
As butterflies dance, hearts flaring.

A squirrel attempts a romantic line,
But the branch breaks, oh what a sign!
The garden with laughter swells and glows,
In springtime's embrace, hilarity flows.

Seeds of Connection

Two seeds met deep in the soil's hug,
One said, "You smell like a big ol' bug!"
The other replied, with roots in a twist,
"At least you don't have that earthy mist!"

They shared their sunlight, grew cheek to cheek,
Chatting and laughing, oh what a peak!
With every sprout, they tickled the ground,
In this quirky patch, true joy is found.

Cascading Petals

Petals tumble down, a juicy delight,
A flower's joke lands with a fluffy fright.
"Why did the bee buzz in my face?"
"To join the party, it's a sweet chase!"

Roses wear their thorns with pride,
While daisies play tag, never hide!
Laughter cascades like a springtime stream,
In this floral realm, life's a funny dream.

The Bloom of Togetherness

In a pot, they chuckle, side by side,
With a succulent wink, they take pride.
"I'm more vibrant than you, don't you know?"
"But I have the best compost to show!"

Together they sprout, with jests and plays,
Creating an oasis of sunny rays.
Their laughter mixed with the fragrant air,
In their quirky world, love's everywhere.

When Sunlight Meets the Soil

A sunflower winks by the garden gate,
It tells the daisies, "Try not to be late!"
The whispers of wind play tag with the leaves,
While ladybugs giggle beneath their green sleeves.

The tomatoes are blushing, they've red cheeks in bloom,
"Did you hear the rumor?" they ask from their gloom.
"That carrot over there, oh what a fine sight!"
"He's got a top hat and he dances at night!"

Nurturing the Unseen

A seed with a dream, so tucked in the ground,
Wonders if today is the day it's unbound.
With a little bit of sunshine and some muddy fun,
It stretches out, grinning, "Oh boy, here I come!"

The worms throw a party, it's quite all the rage,
They dig up some tunes that would brighten the stage.
But the root's been so shy, resting deep, just in case,
It plans a grand entrance with proper sweet grace!

Growth Beneath the Surface

In the dark of the earth, there's a riot of cheer,
As seeds make up odds, like a strange puppet beer.
"Why do we wait?" asks a sprout, feeling bold,
"I'm ready to tell all my secrets untold!"

"Because waiting is fun," said a wise underground sage,
"Just think of the stories we'll share on the stage!"
So they giggled and squirmed, in the cool, damp embrace,

Until one sunny day, they'd all start a race!

A Dance Amongst the Blossoms

The petals all twirl in a flamboyant show,
A bumblebee busts out with a dance-off, you know!
"Don't step on my toes!" yells a daffodil bright,
As tulips applaud with all their flower might.

With each little sway, the garden rocks on,
The clovers tap feet to an old, merry song.
"Come join us, you sprout!" they cry with great glee,
As the blossoms all laugh in their colorful spree!

Raindrops on New Leaves

A little seedling danced with glee,
Its roots were tangled, wild, and free.
It whispered secrets to the sky,
While hoping worms would pass it by.

The raindrops giggled on its head,
"Don't worry, buddy, you'll get fed!"
A beetle joined, it flapped and spun,
Laughing, "Together, we're so fun!"

The sun peeked through, a cheeky grin,
"Look at you growing, let's begin!"
With every splash, the laughter grew,
The garden was a joyous crew.

And so they danced with merry flair,
A botanical circus, without a care.
Each blade of grass rolled with delight,
In this patch of green, love took flight.

An Offering of Petals

A daisy winked at a dandelion,
"Your fluff's so wild, it must be flying!"
The wind giggled, swirling round,
"Oh, what a mess, but how profound!"

The petals blushed a radiant hue,
"Can we be friends? I think it's true!"
With every breeze, they tossed and played,
As butterflies joined, their laughter swayed.

The tulips posed, all prim and neat,
"Don't you know love is quite the feat?"
While violets snickered at the show,
"Get out of here—this isn't a glow!"

But every bloom had love to share,
In gardens deep, with scents so rare.
With every chuckle, colors bright,
They painted joy in morning light.

Echoes of the Heart's Awakening

In the forest, whispers stirred,
A squirrel mumbled, not a word.
"Why do you chirp?" the rabbit asked,
"I'm dreaming of love, it's quite a task!"

The owls hooted, wise and bold,
"Love's just a tale that's often told."
With every rustle, every shout,
They laughed so hard, they flipped about.

A fox tripped over, made a scene,
"Love's a game, if you know what I mean!"
The trees all swayed, a gentle cheer,
For every heartbeat that drew near.

So every creature joined the song,
In the great big woods where dreams belong.
With every laugh, the heart grew bright,
Under the stars, love took flight.

A Soft Embrace in Spring

In springtime's breath, the world awoke,
A bunny snickered, cracked a joke.
"Why did the flower start to sway?"
"It saw the grass and thought, 'Let's play!'"

The sun warmed all with gentle rays,
Bees buzzed close in happy ways.
"Hey, can I borrow your sweet nectar?"
"Sure thing, pal, let's be a spector!"

In every nook, delight took shape,
Like buttercups in every drape.
They danced and twirled, no need to hide,
Joy bubbled up; they laughed, they cried.

As petals fell and laughter soared,
Nature's stage became adored.
With every chuckle, love descended,
A joyful spring that never ended.

Tender Roots of Affection

In gardens where the daisies dance,
Love's seedlings sprout, a glimmering chance.
They twist and twirl in playful delight,
Chasing the bugs on a warm summer night.

With water from giggles and sunshine's grin,
They tangle and titter while growing within.
Silly little hearts in the soil so deep,
Whispering secrets that make the frogs leap.

Awakening Petals

Tiny buds yawn in the morning light,
Stretching their arms, oh what a sight!
They wiggle and giggle, all rosy and bright,
Ordering sunshine, let's dance, take flight!

A bumblebee buzzes, he joins the fun,
"Let's throw a party, oh what a run!"
With pollen confetti, they scatter with glee,
Flowers and laughter, just wait and see!

Nurtured in the Sunlight

Sunbeams sprinkle this lively ground,
Where blushing blooms spin round and round.
They bask in the warmth, a playful parade,
Joking with shadows, a leafy charade.

The roots tell tales with a tangle of fun,
As the vines play tag, oh what a run!
"Catch me if you can," the tulips now cheer,
While dandelions laugh, "We won't disappear!"

Growth Among the Thorns

Among prickly friends, a laugh can be loud,
With roses who jest, they're quite the proud crowd.
"Don't poke us too hard, we've got love to show!"
While thistles chime in, "We steal the show!"

A heart-shaped berry peeks out with a wink,
Sipping sweet nectar, they toast with a clink.
In a patch of mischief, they circle and weave,
Frolicking joy, oh, who wouldn't believe?

Love's Green Symphony

In the garden where giggles bloom,
A kid with a rake, making quite a room.
Sunflowers dance with a silly sway,
Bees buzzing tunes, in a playful ballet.

Planting dreams with seeds of cheer,
We water our hopes; oh my, what a year!
With worms as our band in a compost pit,
We cha-cha through sprouts, never to quit.

A carrot's joke brings a hearty laugh,
As we munch on greens, not do the math.
For in every petal, silliness grows,
Planting smiles wherever love goes.

Budding Promises

Two acorns roll, sharing a jest,
Planning a life with a playful quest.
They promise to grow into mighty trees,
But first, they nap in the summer breeze.

In the shade of petals, we laugh all day,
With dandelion wishes blowing our way.
A rabbit hops in, joins the song,
Chasing his tail, all evening long.

We swap recipes with the squirrels nearby,
For nuts and apples, oh my, oh my!
Fuzzy peach slices drizzled with bliss,
Nature's sweet secret, love's fruity kiss.

Woven From Nature's Embrace

In a tangle of vines, we weave our fate,
A bouquet of giggles, isn't it great?
Ladybugs scatter, wearing tiny hats,
As laughter leaks out from cozy mats.

Chasing the wind in a gopher's race,
Squeaking and squealing, simply a chase.
Nature's own chorus, with joy intertwined,
With roots interlocked, our hearts aligned.

Frilly petals flutter, waving their grace,
Like silly old friends at a lunchbox space.
Sprouts lean in closer, sharing the cheer,
With every green bud, we gather near.

Fertilized by Laughter

In a patch where giggles sprout from the ground,
Miss Daisy laughs, with a hiccuping sound.
Her petals all wrinkled, she sighs with delight,
"Who knew that love bloomed under moonlight?"

Grassy tickles underfoot, oh what joy,
With a garden gnome buddy, quite the ploy.
He holds a sign, 'No funny business here!'
Yet midnight snacks make their antics clear.

With each sprinkle of laughter, we sow hearty tales,
From daisies to dandelions, our joy never fails.
In the compost of friendships, we find and share,
A wacky bouquet of love, beyond compare!

Petals of Affection

In the garden we dance, a whimsical twirl,
You slip on a petal, give me a whirl.
We laugh at the daisies, they giggle back too,
While bees plot their romance, sweet honeydew.

I watered the daisies, you handed me a spade,
Your gardening skills? A charming charade.
The tulips all giggle, they know what they see,
A pair of odd flowers, just you and me.

Butterflies tease us, they flutter and glide,
I tripped on my shoelace, you laughed, full of pride.
With every misstep, our hearts start to bloom,
In this silly garden, there's always room.

So here's to our laughter, like petals in air,
Who needs perfect roses? We've got our own flair.
With roots that grow tangled, we're never apart,
In the garden of chaos, you've captured my heart.

Nurturing the Quiet Glow

In a nook of the night, the stars start to peek,
Your pillow's my throne, your snoring's unique.
We share our sweet secrets, like whispers of light,
As shadows become masters, we giggle in fright.

With blanket fort castles, we plot and we scheme,
Building up dreams like a great, silly dream.
You say I'm the queen, I reply like a gnome,
In this forest of laughter, we've built a fine home.

In each cozy corner, our laughter's a thrill,
You tickle my toes, I'm light as a quill.
With each goofy face, our hearts glow so bright,
In this silly kingdom, we laugh through the night.

So let's chase the shadows, with glee in our stride,
In this wild, fluffy world, let's enjoy the ride.
With each joke a seed, and every grin a tree,
We'll nurture our glow, just you and me.

Rooted in Each Other

Two sprouts intertwined, like twists in a vine,
You say I'm a jokester, I think you're divine.
We giggle like squirrels who just found a nut,
In a world full of chaos, we share a big cut.

Like roots in the soil, we wiggle and sway,
You pretend to be serious, I pretend you're gay.
In this garden of whimsy, we're firm, never weak,
Our laughter's the fertilizer, it's all that we seek.

When storms come a-knocking, we hold on tight,
Spinning in circles, we dance through the night.
With petals of humor, we weather each storm,
In our tangled embrace, we continuously warm.

So let's laugh at the weeds, and the bugs that annoy,
In this playful haven, we'll always find joy.
With roots snug and cozy, we'll never disband,
In the soil of our hearts, together we stand.

Beneath the Canopy of Dreams

Under starlit branches, the blanket we lay,
You whisper a joke, I giggle away.
The moon's a big clown, with a face full of glee,
In our dreamland of fun, it's just you and me.

With fireflies dancing, we make silly plans,
Pretend that we're squirrels, and take quick little scans.
You challenge my wit, I counterattack,
Underneath this green canopy, we've got each other's back.

When the night starts to fade, and our dreams start to stir,
We'll make one last wish, just you and my fur.
Our canopy's humming with laughter and light,
In our silly world, everything feels right.

So let's twirl and let giggles turn into our song,
In this playful union, we always belong.
Beneath this vast sky, with dreams taking flight,
You make every moment sweet laughter in the night.

Hearts Entwined in Nature

Two squirrels dance, a lively sight,
Chasing tails in pure delight.
As nature giggles, blossoms bloom,
Love's sweet scent fills every room.

The bees buzz loud, they sing a tune,
Honey drips beneath the moon.
Flowers wink, dressed in their best,
Nature's folly, love's own jest.

A frog croaks love from lily pads,
While playful ants bring snacks for dads.
The sunbeams tease, they poke and play,
In this world, hearts find their way.

Threads of Light and Love

A pair of socks lost in the wash,
Yet one finds love in the slosh.
Bubbles float with secrets shared,
In laundry's chaos, hearts are paired.

A comet zips across the night,
Leaving trails of pure delight.
Stars giggle in their twinkling flight,
As love takes wing, what a sight!

The kittens chase the laser beam,
Pouncing high in a playful dream.
Each jump's a leap of hearts anew,
A swirling dance 'tween me and you.

A Tapestry of New Life

A wobbly plant stands proud and tall,
In pots of dreams, it dares to sprawl.
Roots deep down, they tickle the dirt,
While leaves above go comically assert.

Two ladybugs share tales so grand,
Of love's adventures across the land.
With every nibble, they laugh and cheer,
Nature's comedy, loud and clear.

The sun sets low, the crickets sing,
Each note a promise, a playful fling.
A tapestry woven by time and chance,
Love grows wild, in nature's dance.

From Soil to Soul

A worm wiggles with style and grace,
Dancing through the dark, muddy space.
He whispers sweet nothings, so sincere,
To flowers that blush, leaning near.

The wind tickles leaves, they giggle and sway,
Chasing sunsets at the end of the day.
With each rustle, they whisper 'my dear',
Nature's jokes tickle hearts, oh so clear.

In this garden, where laughter's the key,
Love sprouts up in the silliest spree.
From soil to soul, together we grow,
A joyous journey, watch us glow.

Tangled in the Foliage

In a garden full of green,
Two hearts giggle, quite unseen.
They tripped on roots, oh what a sight,
Laughter echoes in the night.

Worms did dance beneath their feet,
As they shared some stinky beet.
Bees were buzzing in a buzz,
All the chaos? Just because.

Sun-Kissed Connections

Two tomatoes on the vine,
Chatting about the weather fine.
They joked of salads, dressing bold,
Splashing vinegar, oh so cold.

A carrot rolled and said, "No way!"
"We'll steal the spotlight in the fray."
Lettuce sighed, "What a bizarre show,"
As sunbeams danced, they stole the glow.

Awakening Under the Stars

Under night's sequined quilt,
Two fireflies shared some sweet guilt.
A dance-off broke the silence clear,
They twinkled bright, then disappeared.

"Were you just here?" one bug asked,
"I blinked too fast, it felt unmasked."
The moon chuckled, "You both are daft,
In this glow, you're quite the craft!"

Whispers Among the Leaves

The leaves were gossiping a tale,
Of two squirrels, a clumsy fail.
They chased a nut, so round and red,
And bumped their heads, both thumped and fled.

"Who knew acorns could cause a scene?"
One laughed, feeling rather keen.
With branches swaying in delight,
They made up tales till it was night.

Embraced by Warmth and Light

A seedling peeks from underground,
With sunshine's giggles all around.
It stretches tall, it bends just right,
Can you see it twirl with delight?

A leaf gets tickled by a breeze,
While crickets chirp with playful tease.
They dance and laugh, oh what a sight,
In this garden, hearts take flight!

A bee arrives with a goofy whirr,
He thinks he's smooth, that little blur.
But pollen flies in a funny fight,
Oh dear, the flowers blush bright!

At dusk they wrap in soft embrace,
A moonlit hug, a cutesy grace.
With every laugh, the stars ignite,
Together they twinkle, oh what a night!

The Symphony of New Beginnings

When raindrops fall like clumsy clowns,
They puddle up and make some rounds.
The giggle of grass, so fresh and green,
Says, 'Let's dance – it's time to preen!'

A worm pops up with a startled face,
Joining the plants in a silly race.
They jostle and wiggle, side to side,
As nature's music plays with pride.

A butterfly slips on a blossom's shoe,
A sticky flower – oh, what a hue!
It flutters back, tries to take flight,
But oops! It lands in a patch of white!

With laughter ringing through the air,
The buds break forth, a fragrant flair.
A symphony blooms, oh what a night,
In the garden's joy, all feels just right!

Blossoms in the Heart

In a pot on the porch, two daisies chat,
About the sun and a funny cat.
They giggle and gossip, oh what a start,
Each petal revealing a warm little heart.

The breeze tickles softly, plants sway and sing,
While a ladybug winks, wearing a bling.
With every brush, they share silly sparks,
Creating sweet music, composing their larks.

A tulip trips, a comedic bloom,
Falling face-first in its own perfume.
It laughs off the stumble, shakes off the dirt,
"The world needs more colors; a hint of flirt!"

Together they flourish, laughter their art,
In this vibrant garden, joy's just the start.
With blossoms in tow, they paint the scene,
A charming parade, so bright and serene!

Whispers of New Beginnings

Beneath the soil, a chatter began,
With worms sharing secrets, oh what a plan!
They plotted and schemed, how best to sprout,
To tickle the skies and laugh all about.

A tiny seed chuckled, 'Let's make a scene!'
With acorns and daisies, they formed a dream.
A splash of color, a dash of fun,
They twirled with joy, oh what a run!

When sunshine beamed with a toothy grin,
The blooms burst forth, a colorful spin.
Petals whispered sweetly, secrets to share,
Of newfound feelings floating in air.

They swayed in rhythm, a bright ballet,
With laughter and love leading the way.
In this garden's heart, fun takes its flight,
Whispers of joy make everything right!

Fresh Starts and Fragrant Paths

In the garden of giggles, we play,
With flowers of laughter, bright as the day.
A bee on a mission for honey to find,
Bumbles past roses, leaving us blind.

Sunshine and daisies, we dance in a row,
Each bloom brings a chuckle, where did it go?
A rabbit in slippers hops by with a grin,
Saying, "Join the fun, let the mischief begin!"

Moments like petals drift down all around,
Spreading joy and silliness, laughter unbound.
Each sprout is a secret, a wink and a cheer,
It's a riot of colors, let's give a loud cheer!

With roots intertwined, we bask in the light,
In this garden of humor, we feel so alright.
So plant some wild smiles, watch them all grow,
In a world where love giggles, let's start the show!

A Symphony of Blossoms

In the park where the giggles bloom free,
A symphony plays, can you hear it with glee?
The flowers are dancing, a comical sight,
Even the trees sway with sheer delight.

A squirrel in a bowtie, so dapper and neat,
Jumps into petals, oh what a sweet treat!
The tulips are clapping, standing so tall,
If you listen closely, they're having a ball.

In this patch of delight, with blooms in a rush,
The daisies are gossiping, shushing the hush.
Butterflies slipping, they slip on their shoes,
A tango of colors, bruising the blues.

As we twirl in this upbeat and colorful fray,
The fragrance of joy comes to join in the play.
So giggle with blossoms and sing in the sun,
In this garden of laughter, we're all just having fun!

Delicate Touch of Dawn

At dawn, when the world wears a soft, fluffy hat,
A flower pops up to say, "Hey, how about that?"
A sleepy-eyed daffodil yawns wide with grace,
"Wake up, sleepyheads! Let's start this race!"

With butterflies fluttering in pajamas so bright,
The garden explodes with pure morning light.
Every petal a tale, a chuckle, a tease,
"Don't sit like a button! Get up from your knees!"

As morning unfolds with its giggles and cheer,
The sun winks at daisies, "I brought you good beer!"
A bumblebee buzzes, donning his crown,
"Come join the fun, we'll paint the town brown!"

So tiptoe in dew, let's invite all the fluffs,
To share in this laughter, life's silly little puffs.
In gardens of joy, where the sunlight is drawn,
Let's dance with the petals at the delicate dawn!

Vibrancy in the Air

In a field where the colors play peekaboo,
Nature's shenanigans put on quite the view.
A crocus, a jester, with tricks up his sleeves,
Sprays petals like confetti, oh, how he weaves!

The tulips keep giggling, each one with a grin,
While a shy little poppy tries to sneak in.
With colors so bright, they burst into rhyme,
Singing silly songs, it's party time!

A ladybug loudly declares with delight,
"Join in the fun, let's dance through the night!"
As the sun-light winks, it tickles the air,
Sprouts sway in rhythm, without a care.

So come join the revelry, let colors collide,
In this vibrant frontier, let love be our guide.
With laughter as raindrops, let's splash all around,
In the garden of giggles, pure joy can be found!

Radiance of New Souls

In a garden where giggles bloom,
Two hearts dance, dispelling gloom.
With each glance, a chuckle slips,
Like toddlers with ice cream on their lips.

They trip on vines, then laugh and sway,
Planting seeds in a silly way.
A petal falls, it gives a poke,
In the breeze, a playful joke.

Sunshine giggles, the clouds play tag,
As love grows wild in this sweet rag.
Butterflies tease, with flutters they boast,
While the saplings cheer, raising a toast!

From silly whispers to tangled roots,
In laughter, love's potential shoots.
Each quirky moment, they tenderly weave,
Two playful souls, in joy they believe.

Love's Early Budding

In a patch where clumsy blooms appear,
Two hearts giggle, full of cheer.
Bumblebees buzz with a silly sound,
As they twirl in circles, they can't be found.

Dandelion wishes float in the air,
With every blow, they share a dare.
Hearts tickle, as they blow with glee,
In a race to catch their destiny.

Roots intertwine like spaghetti strands,
In their own little world, they make silly plans.
Love sprouts beneath the silly sun,
Where every glance turns into fun.

With each tickle, new secrets grow,
They giggle at the silliest show.
In this garden of laughter, they find delight,
Playing together from morning till night.

Harvesting the Heartstrings

In fields of dreams, a bounty awaits,
With laughter ringing, joy resonates.
They gather chuckles like ripe sweet fruit,
Every smile a treasure, oh what a hoot!

Their hands fumble as they scoop the sky,
Pinching a cloud for a piece of pie.
In the corn maze, they play hide and seek,
With every corner turned, hearts start to peek.

As they harvest giggles, the air fills bright,
Worms dance in rhythm, it's quite the sight.
Baskets overflow with snickers and grins,
While sunflowers cheer for the playful twins.

With each joyous pluck, they share a treat,
In this silly harvest, life feels complete.
They toast with lemonade, caffeine-free,
In the laughter-filled fields, they dance in glee.

Echoes of Gentle Breezes

Through rustling leaves, their laughter flows,
As they chase butterflies, love sprightly grows.
A breeze trips up the timid trees,
Whispering secrets, carrying ease.

In every flutter, their spirits leap,
With giggly whispers, their hearts keep.
Like a wind-blown kite, they soar and dive,
Chasing giggles, feeling alive.

Twists of vines dance in the air,
As they share thoughts that lead to flair.
Breezes tease, tickling their cheeks,
Bringing joy that simply peaks.

Through echoes of laughter, promises twine,
In the soft whispers, their souls align.
With each gust, love takes its flight,
In a world where breezes stay light.

The Language of Green

In the garden, laughter grows,
Plants tell jokes, as everyone knows.
Roses blush with a little tease,
While daisies giggle in the breeze.

Tomatoes chuckle, ripe and round,
Bamboo sways, keeps time with sound.
Sunflowers wink, so bright and bold,
With secrets of love waiting to unfold.

Veins of Devotion

In the roots, our stories hide,
With wormy friends, we laugh and bide.
A lettuce leaf gives a wink and grin,
While broccoli plans a veggie din.

Cacti roll their spiny eyes,
At lovebirds tangled in sweet ties.
Together we dance, through soil and clay,
In this strange world, come what may.

The Promise of Tomorrow

Tomorrow's seeds, fresh and bright,
Dream of morning's golden light.
Carrots daydream underground,
While mushrooms spread joy all around.

Each sprout whispers its secret wish,
In this odd garden, love's our dish.
Beans climb high, reaching for the sky,
While peas pluck tunes, oh so spry.

Flourishing Together

Side by side, we grow and sway,
In sun and shade, we laugh and play.
A funky dance, we lean and twist,
In this wild patch, none can resist.

The bees hum tunes, as we unite,
In a crazy bouquet, such delight.
Twirling petals, we share our cheer,
In nature's play, love's always near.

Threads of Affection

In the garden of my heart, it seems,
You plant your jokes like funny dreams.
With every chuckle, roots take hold,
Our laughter's worth its weight in gold.

You tease me with your clever puns,
Like two quirky squirrels chasing fun.
In tangled vines, our quirks combine,
A patchwork quilt, oh so divine.

The tiny seedlings sprout with glee,
As we joke 'bout the honey bee.
With every laugh, we grow anew,
In this wild, wacky love we brew.

Among the weeds, our humor thrives,
In this patch, our joy derives.
So raise a toast, let laughter roll,
Thread by thread, we gain our soul.

Where Wildflowers Grow

In a field where daisies dance and sway,
You make me laugh in such a witty way.
Bumblebees buzz, and I'm in a spin,
Watching you trip over tiny stems again.

Your jokes are like the blooms in spring,
Colorful bursts that make my heart sing.
With every smile, the sun starts to glow,
Together we frolic where wildflowers grow.

Pansies wink as we share a jest,
Nearby, the squirrels chuckle at our quest.
We plant the seeds of silly delight,
In the garden of giggles, everything's right.

Through pollen and laughter, we thrive,
In our patch of joy, we feel alive.
Tiny blossoms whisper secrets sweet,
Our love's a bouquet that can't be beat.

The Secret of New Beginnings

When spring arrives, we're in full swing,
Unraveling mysteries the season will bring.
With quirky plans and a wink of fate,
We find humor in every date.

Each giggle's a seed that takes flight,
Planting joy in the soft moonlight.
Our silly mishaps spark new fun,
In this garden, we're never done.

Frogs leap by as we get our cheer,
Whispering secrets that only we hear.
In the chaos, we bloom like the rest,
With playful love, we are truly blessed.

Our laughter echoes, a sweet refrain,
A symphony played in the warm spring rain.
With every chuckle, we start again,
In this delightful dance, joy is our gain.

Lush Dreams and Gentle Caresses

In tangled sheets, we find our play,
With gentle caresses, we chase gray away.
Your giggles tickle, like a soft feather,
In our lush dreams, we stick together.

Each touch, a petal, soft and bright,
Your whispers are cocoa on a chilly night.
We drift in laughter, a warm embrace,
As silly thoughts put smiles on our face.

In the garden of thoughts, we sow our fun,
Chasing sunbeams, never on the run.
With butterflies donning joyful attire,
Our hearts take flight, igniting desire.

Through dreams we wander, hand in hand,
In this laughter-filled, whimsical land.
With every caress, we bloom and expand,
In our world of silly, love's the brand.

Tender Tendrils

We twisted our hands like vines in the air,
Hoping the neighbors won't stop and stare.
With laughter like petals, we danced in the sun,
A tangle of joy, two souls come undone.

Your jokes are like seeds that make my heart bloom,
In the greenhouse of giggles, there's always room.
The garden we tend is wild and a mess,
Yet each little sprout feels like pure happiness.

You prance like a deer with a playful grin,
While I just trip over the tools in the bin.
But through all the chaos, we both still agree,
This lovely little madness is perfect for me.

So let's plant our dreams in pots of delight,
And water with laughter, morning till night.
In this quirky patch where our visions collide,
I'm so glad to have you right here by my side.

A Garden of Shared Dreams

In a plot made of wishes, we dig with our hands,
Each corner adorned with our wild, silly plans.
With dirt on our noses, we craft silly schemes,
In this garden of ours, we're living our dreams.

We water the laughter, it grows like a weed,
And chase away sorrow like a troublesome seed.
Your puns are like sunshine, they brighten the space,
With you in my garden, I've won the best race.

But watch out for gnomes that guard all the fun,
They'll steal all our veggies when we try to run.
Yet every mishap just adds to the cheer,
As we plant all our hopes and grow them right here.

So let's dress in our boots and play in the dirt,
With strawberries sweet and no room for hurt.
In our vibrant Eden, love's color will gleam,
A whimsical world where we're part of a dream.

Fragrant Hopes

With petals of laughter, we scatter our cheer,
Each moment so fragrant, I want you near.
We chase away clouds like pesky old flies,
In this garden of ours, love dances and sighs.

The herbs we plant chuckle, tickling the air,
As we share silly secrets without any care.
Your smile is a flower that blooms in the sun,
With hopes and with giggles, we're never outdone.

The bees stop to giggle at all of our fun,
While butterflies join us; the party's begun!
We fling our ambitions like seeds in a row,
Now let's see what blossoms from love's little show.

With vines intertwining, we dance like two trees,
We sway in the breeze, just as light as you please.
In this fragrant expanse, our spirits will lift,
For in every sweet moment, we've found our true gift.

Crawling Vines of Emotion

Oh, these vines of affection are creeping so fast,
Around every corner, they're tangled at last.
With laughter and giggles that bounce on the ground,
Our garden of feelings is silly, but sound.

We trip on the roots of our dreams as we flail,
As we chase our love's shadow, we both start to wail.
Yet in all of this madness, there's charm to behold,
In this jumbled-up paradise, stories unfold.

The squirrels roll their eyes at our foolish displays,
While grasshoppers hop to the tune of our plays.
With all of this chaos, it's clear to me now,
These crawling green vines have taken a bow.

So let's laugh at the weeds, embrace all the quirks,
And water our dreams with some silly old smirks.
In the garden of hearts where the odd sprouts align,
Oh, what a fine mess, what a wonderful vine!

Whispers of Blooming Hearts

In a garden of giggles, where blooms come alive,
Butterflies chuckle, and bumblebees drive.
With petals so bright, they dance in delight,
While worms in tuxedos plan a grand night.

Roses wear sneakers, tulips sport hats,
Sunflowers gossip about the chubby cats.
The daisies debate how to impress,
But the violets just smile, causing no stress.

They play leapfrog over the fresh green sprouts,
While the daisies shout truths, and laugh out loud shouts.
They twirl 'round the pot, singing tunes on a fling,
As laughter, like pollen, drifts on the wing.

So let's join the laughter, and dance in the air,
In the heart of the garden, there's joy everywhere.
With each funny moment, let's take heart and cheer,
For love is a bloom, that blossoms right here.

The Tender Seedling

A little green seedling whispered with glee,
"I think I'm in love with that big old tree!"
The tree let out a chuckle, a wise old laugh,
"Just watch for the squirrels, they'll steal your path!"

The seedling stood spry, with dreams in its eyes,
Imagining branches that reach for the skies.
"I'll grow tall and strong, with charm and with flair,"
While the roots giggled back, saying, "Take care!"

Days turned to weeks, with sun and some rain,
The seedling got bold, made vows it can't feign.
"Let's dance in the wind, let's sway and twirl bright!"
The tree said, "Just watch out for that kite in flight!"

In joy they would bounce, their laughter would swell,
For love in the garden is a comical spell.
They sprouted together, in light and delight,
With giggles and blooms, they softened the night.

In the Garden of Affection

In the garden of feelings, where laughter does sprout,
All the flowers gather, whispering about.
The roses roll jokes, the lilies do prance,
While the daisies remind them to give love a chance.

A heart-shaped balloon drifts above the sun,
And the veggies are laughing, it's all in good fun.
Cucumbers chuckle, while tomatoes just blush,
As they watch the lovebirds all flutter and gush.

Two frisky ferns flirt in a warm sunny nook,
And the peppers turn red, like the plots in a book.
With giggles and tickles beneath leafy shade,
They plot for a party, fun friendships are made.

So come join the frolic, in this vivid place,
Where love's but a giggle, and joy's the embrace.
With petals and laughter, let's make our mark,
In this playful garden, let's brighten the dark.

Buds in the Dawn

As the sun starts to peek, and the dew drops gleam,
The buds wake up laughing, fresh out of a dream.
With petals all snickering, they sway in the breeze,
While talking of romance among honeybee tease.

"Do you think I'm too green for that charming sprout?"
A shy little daisy quibbles in doubt.
The tulips all chime in, "Oh don't be so coy,
Just dance like a flower, let's spread some joy!"

The morning is ripe with giggles all 'round,
As the plants tell stories of love newly found.
From sunflowers boasting to shy little thyme,
Each bud shares its tales with a rhythm and rhyme.

So gather the blooms for a laugh under dawn,
With humor and heart, let the fun carry on.
For in this sweet garden, with every bright hue,
The buds bloom with laughter, and love feels brand new.

Embracing the New Dawn

The sun pops up, the sky does grin,
Two hearts collide, let the fun begin.
We laugh 'til we cry, it's quite a sight,
Morning coffee spills—oh, what a delight!

Socks mismatched, but who really cares?
We dance in the kitchen, toss up our hairs.
Butterflies tickle, it's all just so silly,
When love grows wild, it can get rather frilly.

Breakfast burnt, the toast turns black,
You giggle so hard, there's no turning back.
With a cherry on top, life's quirky mix,
Let's play through the day, with snacks and quick tricks!

So here's to the dawn, with all its flair,
With breakfast adventures, we've not a care.
Together we'll tumble, take rolls on the grass,
Forever embracing this fun-loving class!

Roots of Connection

Two trees entwined under moon's soft glow,
Their branches flirt, what a charming show!
With roots intertwined, they wiggle with glee,
A dance of the foliage, just wait and see!

Squirrels are laughing, they've joined in the fun,
Making acorn jokes under warmth of the sun.
The grass has confetti; well, why not?
Nature's party is loud, it's quite the hot spot!

When storms blow in, they sway and they shake,
Yet with each raindrop, a joke they'll make.
"Oh look, it's raining!" one tree starts to sing,
"Grab your umbrellas! It's time for bling bling!"

Bound at the roots, they'll weather it all,
With laughter, they rise, no matter the squall.
So, here's to the bond, so playful, so true—
These trees shake it off with a hug and a woo!

Love's Gentle Unfurling

A bud pops open, what's that inside?
Oh, just a secret where giggles reside.
It stretches and yawns, with petals all bright,
And suddenly, sunshine—who turned on the light?

It winks at the daisies, gives them a spin,
Dancing along, with a mischievous grin.
"Oh, do you see that? I'm blooming with flair!"
A flower so cheeky, with blossoms to share.

Nearby a butterfly, with wings all aglow,
Says, "Oh my, darling, your confidence grows!"
She flutters and teases, a flirty ballet,
In this garden of laughter, we twirl and sway.

With bees buzzing 'round, it's humorous fate,
They come for the nectar, and dance on a plate.
Together we grow, it's a whimsical show,
Unfurling the fun, in this garden we sow!

Petals Swaying in the Breeze

With petals a-dance, they swish and they sway,
Two roses trade jokes in the light of the day.
A honeybee chuckles at their playful spat,
"Don't let the gardener hear—he might feel flat!"

The daffodils bob, like they're in a parade,
With sunshine as spotlight, they've all got it made.
"Did you hear the one about the tulip and dew?"
Banter flows freely, their friendship rings true.

As breezes tickle, they share all their dreams,
Running wild in the garden, or so it seems.
"Climb up this trellis, let's reach for the stars,
And find out if we can plant laughter on Mars!"

With whispers of wind, they giggle and spin,
These petals, so lively, can't help but grin.
So here's to the moments, so silly and bright,
In this floral ballet, they twirl with delight!

From Bud to Blossom

In the garden of giggles, we start to grow,
Petals unfolding, putting on a show.
With a wink and a nudge, we dance in the breeze,
Spraying each other with water—oh, such tease!

Bees buzzing by with a curious hum,
They pause for a moment, then join in the fun.
A flower hat here, a bouquet for the queen,
We'll laugh till we drop—what a silly scene!

Worms tell jokes while the daisies all sway,
Petunias gossip about the compost bay.
With each playful tickle, we're growing, oh dear,
Let's plant a few puns in this soil full of cheer!

In this patch of delight, we'll bloom and we'll jest,
Every leaf a giggle, every bud a quest.
When we're finally ripe, under sunshine we'll sway,
Together we blossom in our comical way!

Soft Rain on New Growth

Raindrops are falling, a slick little dance,
Tickling each sprout, giving life a chance.
A puddle's a mirror, reflecting our glee,
Let's splash in the fun, just you and me!

Each droplet a laugh, our worries all flee,
Like seedlings we wriggle, so wild and so free.
Our roots intertwine, like best friends do share,
With water fights brewing, we toss without care!

The sun peeks out too, a cheeky old friend,
Who joins in the laughter, the fun knows no end.
With mud on our faces, we roll without shame,
In this garden of joy, we'll never be tame!

So let's dance in the rain, while the flowers take note,
Of our silly antics afloat like a boat.
Tomorrow, we'll sprout in more playful array,
Under soft rain, let's grow wild in our play!

Colors of Desire

In the palette of spring, our colors collide,
With fuchsia and lime, we are bursting with pride.
A daisy in polka dots, how can we resist?
When humor's in bloom, it's hard to stay missed!

Scarlet petunias squat, competing to flaunt,
While lavender giggles, making jokes that don't haunt.
With colors so loud, we'll paint the whole patch,
Every bud has a style, an unforgettable match!

Yellow sunflowers winking, oh what a sight,
Disguised as the sun, they bring giggles so bright.
In the garden of whimsy, we dance and we swirl,
Our hearts paint the canvas of this quirky world!

From vibrant wildflowers to shy violets' peek,
We bloom in our hues with laughter we speak.
So come take a stroll through this riot of cheer,
In the colors of joy, we're forever sincere!

Emerge with the Dawn

As the sun starts to peek, we awake with a yawn,
Stretching our petals, emerging with dawn.
Through sleepy chuckles, the morning takes flight,
With giggles and grins, we're fresh and so bright!

The dew on the leaves, like twinkling champagne,
Makes the world feel alive with a sprinkle of rain.
While morning glories wrap around in a hug,
We stumble together, a laughter-filled rug!

Bugs on parade with their wiggly moves,
Join the potluck breakfast of laughs and grooves.
In the charm of the morning, we sway side to side,
Underneath all the petals, we chuckle with pride!

Emerge with the dawn, as the day jumps awake,
With a burst of delight, there's no room for fake.
With blossoms and banter, we'll face what's ahead,
Let's bloom in good humor, for joy's always spread!

www.ingramcontent.com/pod-product-compliance
Lightning Source LLC
Chambersburg PA
CBHW070314120526
44590CB00017B/2677